The Cat Burglar

Written and illustrated by Nicola Senior

Collins

Chapter 1

Bea lived with her cat, Peaches.

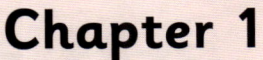

Peaches spied on the avenue, keeping a lookout from her seat. She kept still, looking around the skies and gardens with interest.

A magpie hopped onto a garden bench and grabbed a blue unicorn that had been left.

Peaches looked at Bea. Had she seen it?
No, Bea was enjoying her beans on toast.

Crouched on her seat, Peaches spotted the magpie flap its wings and disappear.

She sighed and went back to sleep.

Chapter 2

Peaches continued to look out. Carlotta was in her garden, drinking tea as she fed the birds. She put the teacup down and forgot about it.

The magpie swooped it away.

Peaches looked around. Had Bea seen it?
No, Bea was reading a book. Peaches sat up.
She had a clever plan.

Chapter 3

When the magpie next appeared, it had a scarf. Peaches had seen Irwin from across the street with a scarf just like it. Had the magpie pinched it?

Peaches had to act now.

That night, Peaches checked a streetmap.

She planned to steal the objects back from the magpie, and return them to the right person.

Chapter 4

Peaches bounded along the rooftops in the moonlight, keeping a lookout for the missing things.

She spotted a high tree.

A scarf had been wound around the tree like a nest. In the nest, there was a unicorn and Carlotta's teacup.

Peaches continued all night. She rescued each thing and took them back in her mouth.

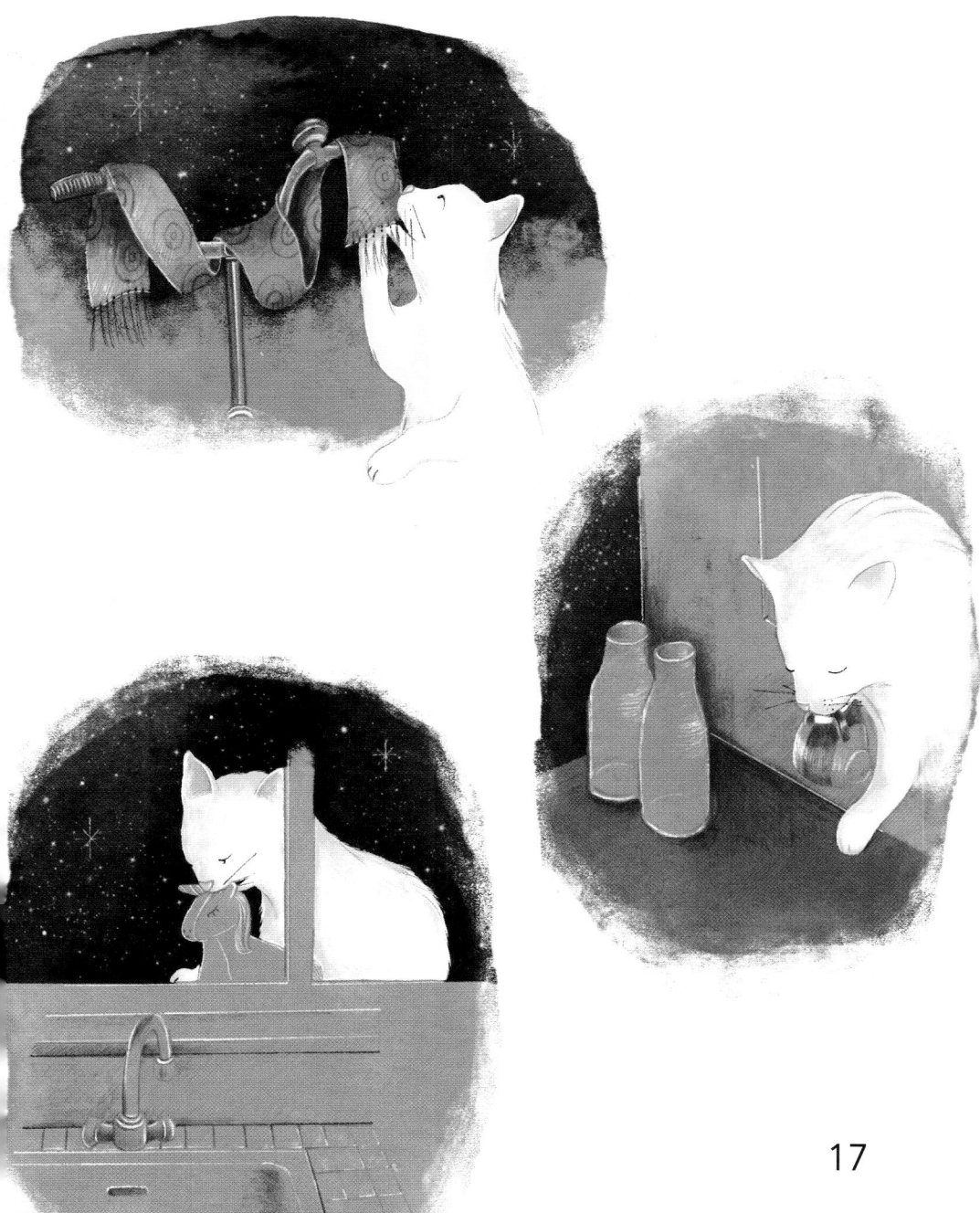

Chapter 5

Irwin was glad.

May hugged her unicorn.

"My teacup!" cried Carlotta. "But how did it come back?"

The next week, Bea was telling Joy all about it. "I still do not understand it. What do you think, Peaches? Do you have a clue?"

Bea and Joy hooted.

As if Peaches had a clue!

She was just a cat and slept all day long!

Didn't she?

Peaches' plan

What did the magpie steal?

Magpie facts

- Magpies are clever birds.

- Real magpies do not often steal things.

- Magpie nests can have a roof!

The cat burglar

Review: After reading

Use your assessment from hearing the children read to choose any GPCs, words or tricky words that need additional practice.

Read 1: Decoding
- Ask the children to look for these words and explain them in context.
  page 10 **pinched** (*stole*)   page 15 **spotted** (*saw, noticed*)
- Can the children hear whether there's an /oo/ or /yoo/ sound in these words?
  avenue (/yoo/)   **clue** (/oo/)   **rescued** (/yoo/)
  unicorn (/yoo/)   **blue** (/oo/)
- Model reading pages 2 and 3 fluently without pausing. Then point to words on these pages at random, saying: Try to blend in your head when you read these words.

Read 2: Prosody
- Turn to pages 18 and 19. Focus on the punctuation and how it guides the reader to read with expression.
  o Point to the exclamation mark on page 18. Ask: What feeling can you put into your voice when you read this sentence?
  o Point to the commas on page 19, and explain that they make the reader pause. Encourage the children to read page 19, pausing at the commas.
  o Ask: Did you notice the question marks? Can you read these sentences to make them sound more like questions? Encourage the children to reread the page.
- Bonus content: Turn to pages 28 and 29. Challenge the children to read the pages as if they were a broadcaster on television. How exciting can they make the facts sound?

Read 3: Comprehension
- Talk about the cat. Discuss whether they think this is a typical cat. Ask: Do you know of any cats that seem to watch and listen? Do you think real cats are as clever as this cat in the book? Why?
- Focus on the title and say: A "cat burglar" is a real term for people who are burglars, and steal from houses by climbing up walls and through windows. Why do you think burglars like that are called "cat burglars"? (*They move and climb like a cat.*)
- Reread pages 20 to 23. Ask:
  o Do Bea and Joy know what Peaches has been doing? How do you know? (*No. They are joking about the fact that she is just a cat.*)
  o Discuss a different sort of ending for their story – in which Bea and Joy discover that Peaches isn't clueless after all.
- Turn to pages 30–31, and encourage the children to retell the story in their own words using the pictures as prompts.
- Bonus content: Turn to pages 26 and 27. Ask the children to make up more details for one of the characters, describe them and explain why their object is important to them.